*STYLE IT: TRENDS AND FADS

SHOE SAVVY

by VIRGINIA LOH-HAGAN

# 45TH PARALLEL PRESS

Published in the United States of America by
Cherry Lake Publishing Group
Ann Arbor, Michigan
www.cherrylakepublishing.com

Reading Adviser: Beth Walker Gambro, MS, Ed., Reading Consultant, Yorkville, IL
Book Designer: Joseph Hatch

Photo Credits: Melvin Buezo/Pexels.com, cover; Jamaal Hutchinson/Pexels.com, 4; Mestos, CC BY-SA 3.0 via Wikimedia Commons, 7; I, Daniel Schwen, CC BY-SA 3.0 via Wikimedia Commons, 8; © Bigshow Lamar Campton/Shutterstock, 11; Caco Portela/Pexels.com, 13; © Kostikova Natalia/Shutterstock, 14; Mizuno K/Pexels.com, 16; © Wsluvvv/Shutterstock, 19; Jayson Hinrichsen/Pexels.com, 21; Photographer: obedms, CC BY 2.0 via Wikimedia Commons, 22 (top); © NYCKellyWilliams/Shutterstock, 22 (bottom); MelikeB/Pexels.com, 24; Liza Summer/Pexels.com, 27; William Warby/Pexels.com, 28; Ingo Joseph/Pexels.com, 30; Kheel Center, CC BY 2.0 via Wikimedia Commons, 31

Copyright © 2026 by Cherry Lake Publishing Group

All rights reserved. No part of this book may be reproduced or utilized in any form or by any means without written permission from the publisher.

**45th Parallel Press** is an imprint of Cherry Lake Publishing Group.

Library of Congress Cataloging-in-Publication Data

Names: Loh-Hagan, Virginia, author.
Title: Shoe savvy / written by Virginia Loh-Hagan.
Description: Ann Arbor, Michigan : 45th Parallel Press, [2025] | Series: Style it : trends and fads | Includes bibliographical references. | Audience: Grades 7-9 | Summary: "Shoe savvy was prized way back when and it still is now! Take a look at the modern and historical trends and fads that have come and gone in the world of footwear. Readers of these hi-lo books will be surprised by various trends and fads that will keep them guessing until the very end"— Provided by publisher.
Identifiers: LCCN 2025009133 | ISBN 9781668963845 (hardcover) | ISBN 9781668965160 (paperback) | ISBN 9781668966778 (ebook) | ISBN 9781668968383 (pdf)
Subjects: LCSH: Shoes—Juvenile literature. | Fashion design—History—Juvenile literature.
Classification: LCC TT678.5 .L64 2025 | DDC 685/.3102—dc23/eng/20250423
LC record available at https://lccn.loc.gov/2025009133

Cherry Lake Publishing Group would like to acknowledge the work of the Partnership for 21st Century Learning, a Network of Battelle for Kids. Please visit Battelle for Kids online for more information.

Note from publisher: Websites change regularly, and their future contents are outside of our control. Supervise children when conducting any recommended online searches for extended learning opportunities.

Printed in the United States of America

**Dr. Virginia Loh-Hagan** is an author and educator. She is currently the Executive Director for Asian American Native Hawaiian Pacific Islander Affairs at San Diego State University and the Co-Executive Director of The Asian American Education Project. She lives in San Diego with her very tall husband and very naughty dogs.

# TABLE of CONTENTS

**INTRODUCTION** ......................................... 5

CHAPTER 1: **Lotus Shoes** ....................... 9

CHAPTER 2: **Men's High Heels** ...............10

CHAPTER 3: **Wooden Klomps** ...............12

CHAPTER 4: **Crakows**..............................15

CHAPTER 5: **Ballet Slippers** ...................17

CHAPTER 6: **Split-Toe Shoes** .................18

CHAPTER 7: **Sneakers** ........................... 20

CHAPTER 8: **Mexican Pointy Boots**....... 23

CHAPTER 9: **Crocs** ................................. 25

CHAPTER 10: **Furry Footwear**................ 26

**DO YOUR PART!** ..................................... 29

**GLOSSARY**............................................. 32

**LEARN MORE** ........................................ 32

**INDEX**................................................... 32

**There are always new shoe trends! Which ones have you seen lately?**

# Introduction

Everybody has style. Some people have more style than others. They stand out. They use **fashion** to express themselves. Fashion is about how people want to look. It's about how people dress. It includes clothes, shoes, hats, and jewelry. It also includes hairstyles and makeup.

Fashion changes across cultures. It changes over time. There are many fashion **trends**. Trends are fads. They're patterns of change. They reflect what's popular at a certain time. Many people copy popular looks. They copy famous people. They get inspired. They want to be cool. They want to be in style.

Some trends last a long time. Other trends are short. All trends make history.

Shoes serve a purpose. We wear shoes when we walk. Shoes protect our feet. They support our feet. But they can be more than just useful. They add to our style. They add beauty. They add personality. They play a key role in fashion.

People have worn all types of shoes. Shoes come in all shapes. They come in all sizes. They come in all colors. Some people have fun with their shoes. Some even collect them!

Some shoes are fancy. Some are simple. There have been a lot of different shoe trends. This book features some of the fun ones!

The oldest known shoes were made from bark. They date back to 10,000 years ago.

Today, lotus shoes are collected. They're works of art. They're artifacts.

# CHAPTER One

## Lotus Shoes

From 960 to the early 1900s, some Chinese women wore **lotus** shoes. These shoes looked like lotus flower buds. They were praised for being small. They were made of silk. They were handcrafted. They had pretty designs. Women added personal touches. They showed off their sewing skills.

Lotus shoes were a result of foot binding. Women wanted small feet. Small feet were a sign of beauty. They were a sign of social class. Young girls' feet were wrapped with cloth. This forced toes to bend under. It broke bones. It made feet small and pointy. This practice was banned in 1911. It's dangerous. Women couldn't move easily. Some got sick. Some even died.

CHAPTER

# TWO

# Men's High Heels

Persia was the former name of Iran. In the 10th century, Persian men were the first to wear high heels. High heels helped them ride horses. They kept their feet in the **stirrups**. These are loops or rings that hang from the sides of a saddle. Stirrups helped riders stay in saddles. The heels made riders more stable. This allowed them to shoot bows and arrows.

These heeled boots were called *galesh*. They were made by hand. They were covered in leather. They had metal bands on the heels. They became a symbol of money and power.

Persian soldiers traded with other countries. This spread the trend of men wearing high heels. European kings loved them. They copied the look.

# FASHION-FORWARD PIONEER

Adam King is an Asian American. He has worked for many shoe companies. He founded 1587 Sneakers in 2023. 1587 Sneakers has said it is "the first U.S. sneaker brand whose mission is to celebrate culture and tell authentic AAPI stories." 1587 is the year Asians first arrived in what is today the United States. King said, "Asian Americans are amazing sneaker consumers. They're 8% of the population. But they're like 14% of sales." It upset King that companies didn't market to Asian Americans. He saw an opportunity. He partnered with Sam Hyun. Hyun is a popular social **activist**. Activists fight for change. They want a better world. King also thought he was "super fashionable and handsome." 1587 sneakers are a hit. They're simple, elegant, and well-made. King wants kids to equate "cool" with "Asian American culture."

Many 1587 Sneakers shoes are white with a pop of color.

CHAPTER

# THREE

# **Wooden Klomps**

Clogs have thick, rigid soles. They're usually made of wood. Versions have existed since ancient times. But the most famous came from the Netherlands. They're called Dutch klomps. These shoes can be traced to the 1300s. They were made from a single wood block.

At first, **peasants** wore klomps. Peasants were people of low social status. They didn't have much money. The shoes were cheap. They were meant to be worn every day. They were good for fieldwork. They were good for factory work. They protected feet from sharp objects. They also protected feet from getting wet.

Later, they became a trend. Rich people wore them. In the 1800s, they started to be used for dancing.

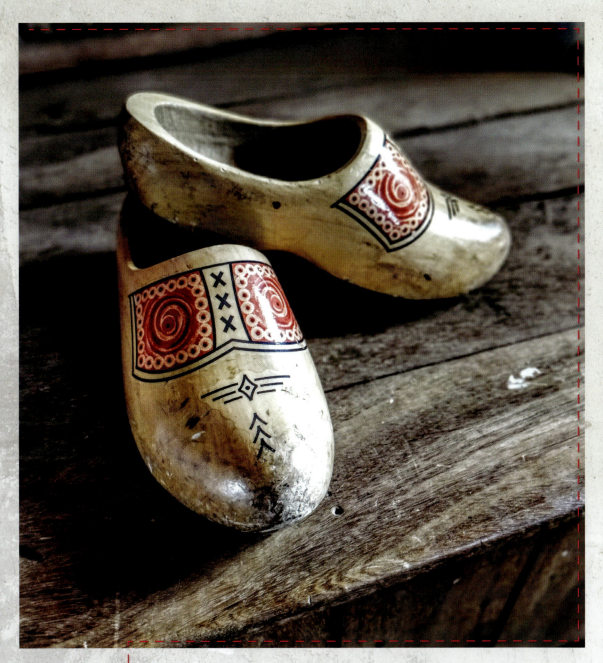
Some people paint wooden clogs. This makes them more stylish.

# FASHION REBEL: TRENDSETTER

Flor de María Rivera was born in Peru. She worked in sports broadcasting. Then she switched to fashion. She hosted a bilingual fashion blog. She wrote about her love for shoes. She owned more than 500 pairs. But she was still missing the perfect pair. She wanted pretty shoes that she could wear all day long. So she designed her own shoes. Her shoes are comfortable. They're stylish. They're high-quality. She launched her company in 2019. Famous people such as Kylie Jenner and Jenna Ortega wear her shoes. Rivera said, "I draw inspiration from the fearless females in my life." She is focused on empowering women. She bases her company in San Francisco, California.

CHAPTER

## FOUR

# Crakows

**Crakows** were made of leather. They were long, skinny, pointy shoes. Some points were over 20 inches (50.8 centimeters) long. They were stuffed with moss or wool. This helped retain the shape.

Crakows originated in Krakow, Poland. They spread to the rest of Europe. They were popular in the 14th and 15th centuries. Mainly rich people wore them. Both men and women wore them.

Crakows caused foot pain. They made people fall. They made it hard for people to kneel and pray. Some Christians thought the shoes were vain. They thought they were sinful.

King Charles V was the king of France. In 1368, he banned them. Almost a hundred years passed. King Edward IV was then the king of England. In 1463, he banned them. Shoe points couldn't be over 2 inches (5 cm) long.

Today, wearing ballet flats is a classic look. They're simple and elegant.

CHAPTER

# Five

# Ballet Slippers

Ballet dancers wear ballet slippers. These shoes are light. They're made from soft leather, fabric, or satin. They're flexible. They're often pink or black. Today, dancers wear skin-colored slippers. Some ballet slippers have special toes. The toes help feet stand on point.

Ballet dancing started in the 1400s. Ballet shoes at this time had heels. Marie Camargo was a French dancer. In the 1700s, she was the first to wear slippers. She was able to dance more freely. This inspired other dancers to wear slippers as well.

Salvatore Capezio was an Italian shoemaker. He had a shop across from an opera house. He repaired ballet shoes. Soon, he was selling them. That was in the 1940s. They became a fashion trend. Everyone wanted a pair! They're comfortable. They're pretty.

## Chapter Six

# Split-Toe Shoes

**Tabi shoes** are traditional Japanese footwear. They have a split between the big toe and the other toes. They were made from a single animal **hide**. Hides are animal skins.

The split-toe design emerged around the 11th century. Tabi socks allowed people to also wear sandals. Tabi shoes allowed warriors to stand strong on battlefields. They provided more support. The split toe provided more comfort.

The Ishibashi brothers founded Bridgestone. They were the world's largest makers of tires. They invented tabi shoes with rubber soles. They did this in 1922. These tabi shoes could be used outdoors. They could be used for sporty activities. They became widely popular.

# DIY FASHION FUN

You can buy fun socks most places. Choose a pattern that makes you smile!

**ADD SOME SASS TO YOUR SHOES. HERE ARE SOME IDEAS:**

» With an adult's permission, draw designs on your shoes. Use markers, pens, paints, or threads. People today like to customize things. They like to make things their own. Many shoes are made of fabric. It's easy to add your own flair to fabric.

» Use ribbons instead of shoelaces. Use pastel colors. This will add a "cottagecore" vibe. This look is soft and pretty. It reminds people of being in the country.

» Wear fun socks. Socks protect feet from blisters. They keep feet dry. But they can also up your shoe game. Fun socks get noticed. They are trendy. Today, they can even be worn at work.

## CHAPTER SEVEN

# Sneakers

Sneakers are also called trainers, runners, kicks, or tennis shoes. They have rubber soles. Rubber made the shoes quiet. Wearers could "sneak" around. That's why sneakers are called sneakers.

Sneakers are designed for sports. They have flexible soles. They have tread for grip. They can absorb impact. They're good for running, dancing, and jumping.

But today, they're a fashion trend. They're worn all day long. They're worn by everyone. **Sneakerheads** love sneakers. They wear sneakers. They collect sneakers. They trade sneakers. They talk about sneakers. They go to sneaker events. Sneakerhead culture formed in the 1980s. It was inspired by basketball and hip-hop music. It's still around today.

Today, all-white sneakers are still hot. They can be worn with any outfit. Also, chunky sneakers are back!

CHAPTER EIGHT

# Mexican Pointy Boots

The pointy trend keeps coming back. Around 2002, Mexican pointy boots emerged in Mexican resort towns. They were worn by men.

The boots made their appearance at big festivals, rodeos, and clubs. They were part of the local electronic music scene. Performers wore them first. Then other people wore them. They become popular in the 2010s. This trend spread to states close to the border.

These boots had long toes. Some toes were 5 feet (1.5 meters) long. They curled up toward the knees. The boots were decorated. People added designs. They added glitter. They added flashing lights. They added many fun things.

**Some Mexican pointy boots have been shown at museums.**

Today, people add Jibbitz to their Crocs. Jibbitz are charms.

CHAPTER

nine

# Crocs

Crocs are comfortable, ugly shoes. They're also a huge hit. They were invented in 2002. Three friends went on a boating trip. They were inspired to improve boating shoes. They added a heel strap. This kept shoes from falling off. Crocs have holes on top. This helps air circulate. It lets sweat escape.

Crocs are named after crocodiles. They are made from special plastic. They're light. They can be used for many purposes. They can be worn on land. They can be worn in water. They're just like crocodiles.

Crocs were a big thing in the early 2000s. But this fad slowed down. But in 2020, people were in lockdown. Many worked from home. They wanted comfort. Crocs came back.

CHAPTER

Ten

# Furry Footwear

Fashion trends are not just about what looks good. Some designers seek to bring in the ugly and the weird. There's a new ugly shoe trend in town. Furry footwear is here.

There are furry heels. There are furry flip-flops. There are furry boots. There are even furry sneakers. Some shoes are furry all over. Some just have fur trim.

Fur lining in shoes started in ancient times. It traps heat. It keeps feet warm. It's soft. It's comfortable. It keeps feet dry. But today's designers are moving fur from the inside to the outside. Fur, feathers, fluff, and fuzz are high culture. Will this trend last? How will it change? We shall see!

Today, UGG® boots are still the go-to cozy shoes. They were invented in the 1970s.

**Americans throw away 300 million pairs of shoes each year.**

# DO YOUR PART!

It's always fashionable to stand up for what's right. Fashion can be more than just about looks. It can be used to fight for causes. Be a fashion activist. Here are some ways to make a difference:

- Buy **cruelty-free**, **vegan** shoes. This means no animals were harmed or used. Don't buy shoes made of leather, wool, or silk. Instead, buy shoes made from plants. This includes corn, bamboo, or fabric. Some shoes are even made from recycled plastics. Protect animals while still wearing great shoes.

- Wear the same shoes a lot. Don't buy a lot of shoes. Making shoes takes up a lot of energy and water. It adds chemicals to the air. It pollutes the air. This can be bad for nature. Own a few great pairs of shoes. Do more with less. Save the planet.

- Donate your shoes. Consider buying lightly used shoes. Buy shoes made of recycled materials. Shoes take up space in **landfills**. Landfills are places that bury waste. Shoes take many years to **decompose**. Decompose means to break down.

- Remember, every little bit counts. Kindness matters. You can look good and feel great!

Feel like you want to be a fashion activist? Find some friends to join you!

# FIGHTING FOR JUSTICE

## Shopping for shoes is not an equal experience for everyone.

From the 1860s to 1960s, the U.S. South had Jim Crow laws. These laws enforced racist policies. They enforced segregation. They discriminated against Black Americans. For example, Black Americans had to shop in separate areas. They couldn't try on shoes at stores. They had to know their exact shoe sizes. They had to buy shoes based on that. They couldn't return shoes. White store owners worried that White customers wouldn't buy shoes worn by Black people. Many Black activists fought against racism. The Civil Rights Movement of the 1960s helped pass laws that ended the Jim Crow era.

# Glossary

**activist** (AK-tih-vist) person who fights for political or social change

**crakow** (KRAA-koh) shoe, boot, or slipper with long pointed toe from the 14th and 15th centuries

**cruelty-free** (KROOL-tee-FREE) free from animal testing

**decompose** (dee-kuhm-POHZ) to decay or break up into smaller parts

**fashion** (FAA-shuhn) any way of dressing that is favored or popular at any one time or place

**hide** (HIYD) skin of an animal that has been treated for human use

**landfills** (LAND-filz) places to bury trash and waste material

**lotus** (LOH-tuhs) large water lily flower

**peasants** (PEH-zuhnts) people of a low social status and less money in a society

**sneakerheads** (SNEE-kuhr-hedz) people with expert knowledge about sneakers who collect and trade sneakers as a hobby

**stirrups** (STUHR-uhps) loops or rings that hang from the sides of a saddle

**tabi shoes** (TAY-bee SHOOZ) traditional Japanese footwear with a split between the big toe and other toes

**trends** (TRENDZ) fads or changes that are popular or common

**vegan** (VEE-guhn) containing no animal products

# Learn More

Galbraith, Melissa. *DIY Embroidered Shoes: Techniques, Designs, and Downloadable Templates to Turn Any Fabric Shoe into Stylish & Unique Footwear.* Mount Joy, PA: Landauer Publishing, 2024.

Hoena, Blake. *Sneakers: A Graphic History.* Minneapolis, MN: Lerner Publishing, 2021.

Wood, Simon. *The Ultimate Sneaker Book.* Los Angeles, CA: Taschen America LLC, 2024

# Index

animal materials, 15, 18, 26
art and artifacts, 8
athletic shoes, 11, 18, 20–21

ballet slippers, 16–17
boots, 10, 22–23, 27

consumer ethics, 28–31
crakows, 15
creating and crafting, 19
Crocs, 24–25
cruelty-free shoes, 29
cultural details, 9–12, 15, 17–18, 20, 23, 31

fashion, 5–6
fashion and shoe designers, 11, 14, 17
1587 Sneakers (brand), 11
foot binding, 9
formality and status of shoes, 8–10, 12, 20

functionality of shoes, 6, 9–10, 12, 17–18, 20, 25–26
furry footwear, 26–27

high-heeled shoes, 10, 14
Hyun, Sam, 11

King, Adam, 11

lotus shoes, 8–9

marketing and market share, 11
materials, 6–7, 10, 12–13, 15, 17–18, 20, 25–26, 29
men's high heels, 10
Mexican pointy boots, 22–23

personal style, 5–6, 11, 20, 23

racism, 31
Rivera, Flor de María, 14

safety issues, 9, 12, 15
segregation, 31
shoes, 4–6, 8–12, 14–15, 17–20, 25–31
sneakers, 11, 20–21
socks, 18–19
split-toe shoes, 18
structures of shoes, 8–10, 15, 17–18, 20, 22–23, 25–26
sustainability, 28–30

tabi shoes, 18
trends, 4–5, 8–10, 12–13, 15–18, 20–27

UGG® boots, 27

vegan shoes, 29

waste, 28, 30
wooden klomps, 12–13